Wenceslas

A Christmas Poem

Carol Ann Duffy

Illustrated by Stuart Kolakovic

PICADOR

First published 2012 by Picador
An imprint of Pan Macmillan, a division of Macmillan Publishers Limited
Pan Macmillan, 20 New Wharf Road, London N1 9RR
Basingstoke and Oxford
Associated companies throughout the world
www.panmacmillan.com

ISBN 978-1-4472-1202-7

A CIP catalogue record for this book is available from
the British Library.

Manufactured in Belgium by Proost

Visit *www.picador.com* to read more about all our books
and to buy them. You will also find features, author interviews and
news of any author events, and you can sign up for e-newsletters
so that you're always first to hear about our new releases.

For Barry, Rachel and Anna
in loving memory of Tricia

Wenceslas

he King's Cook had cooked for the King
a Christmas Pie,

wherein the Swan,
once bride of the river,
half of for ever,
six Cygnets circling her,
lay scalded, plucked, boned, parboiled,
salted, peppered, gingered, oiled;

and harboured the Heron
whose grey shadow she'd crossed
as it stood witness,

                grave as a Priest,

on the riverbank.

Now the Heron's breast was martyred with Cloves.

Inside the Heron inside the Swan –
in a greased cradle, pastry-sealed –
a Common Crane,

                        gutted and trussed,
smeared with Cicely, Lavender, Rose,
was stuffed with a buttered, saffroned
golden Goose.

       Within the Goose,
perfumed with Fruits, was a Duck,
and jammed in the Duck, a Pheasant,
embalmed in Honey

                from Bees

                        who'd perused

the blossoms of Cherry trees.

Spring in deep midwinter;

a year in a pie;

a Guinea-Fowl in a Pheasant;

a Teal in a Fowl.

Nursed in the Teal,
a Partridge, purse to a Plover;
a Plover, glove to a Quail;
and caught in the mitt of the Quail,

a Lark –

a green Olive stoppered its beak.

The Christmas Pie
for the good King, Wenceslas,
was seasoned with Sage, Rosemary, Thyme;
and a living Robin sang through a hole in its crust.

Pot-herbs to accompany this;
Roasted Chestnuts, Red Cabbage,
Celery, Carrots, Colly-flowre,
each borne aloft by a Page
                            into the Hall,
where the Pie steamed on a table
in front of the fire;

                    and to flow at the feast,
mulled Wine, fragrant
with Nutmeg, Cinnamon, Mace,
with Grains of Paradise.
                              The Lords and Ladies
sat at their places, candlelight
on their festive faces.

Up in the Minstrels' Gallery,
the King's Musicians tuned the Lute
to the Flute
          to the Pipe
to the Shawm, the Gemshorn, the Harp,
to the Dulcimer
              to the Psaltery;
and the Drum was a muffled heart
like an imminent birth
and the Tambourine was percussion as mirth.

Then a blushing Boy stood to trill
of how the Beasts, by some good spell,
in their crude stable began to tell
the gifts they gave Emmanuel.

Holly, Ivy, Mistletoe,

shredded Silver,

hung from the rafters

and the King's Fool
                        pranced beneath
five red Apples,
                  one green Pear,
which danced in the air.

Snow at the window twirled;
and deep, crisp, even,

        covered the fields
where a fox and a vixen curled in a den
as the Moon scowled
at the cold, bold, gold glare of an Owl.

Also there,
  out where the frozen stream
lay nailed to the ground,
was a prayer
  drifting as human breath,
as the ghost of words,
  in a dark wood,
yearning to be
  Something
  Understood.

But Heaven was only old light
and the frost was cruel
where a poor, stooped man

                    went gathering fuel.

A miracle then,

                fanfared in,

that the King in red robes, silver crown,

glanced outside

                from his wooden throne

to see the Pauper

                stumble, shiver,

and sent a Page to fetch him
Hither.

Then Wenceslas sat the poor man down,
poured Winter's Wine,
and carved him a sumptuous slice

of the Christmas Pie . . .

as prayers hope You would, and I.

Also by Carol Ann Duffy and available from Picador